Be Safe!

Bicycle Safety

by Peggy Pancella

Heinemann Library
Chicago, Illinois

Customer Service 888-454-2279
Visit our website at www.heinemannlibrary.com

Designed by Heinemann Library
Page layout by Roslyn Broder
Printed and bound in China by South China Printing Co. Ltd.

09 08 07 06
10 9 8 7 6 5 4 3 2

Library of Congress Cataloging-in-Publication Data
Pancella, Peggy.
  Bicycle safety / Peggy Pancella.
      v. cm. -- (Be safe!)
  Includes bibliographical references and index.
  Contents: What is safety? -- Choosing a bike -- Helmets -- Checking your equipment -- Dressing for safety -- Safe places to ride -- Rules of the road -- Hand signals -- Crossing streets -- Dangers on the road -- Ride with care -- If you fall -- Bicycle fun -- Safety tips.
  ISBN 1-4034-4930-9 (hardcover) -- ISBN 1-4034-4939-2 (pbk.)
  1. Cycling--Safety measures--Juvenile literature. 2. Bicycles--Safety measures--Juvenile literature. [1. Bicycles and bicycling--Safety measures. 2. Safety.] I. Title.
  GV1055.P36 2003
  796.6'028'9--dc22

                              2003024062

Acknowledgments
The author and publisher are grateful to the following for permission to reproduce copyright material:
Cover photograph by Anthony Redpath/Corbis
pp. 4, 7, 8, 9, 11, 15, 18, 19, 26, 27 Greg Williams/Heinemann Library; pp. 5, 23 Corbis; p. 6 Bonnie Kamin/PhotoEdit, Inc.; pp. 10, 13, 14, 20 David Young-Wolff/PhotoEdit, Inc.; p. 12 Richard Hutchings/Corbis; p. 16 Michael Newman/Photo Edit, Inc.; p. 17 Davis Barber/PhotoEdit, Inc.; p. 21 Cindy Charles/PhotoEdit, Inc.; p. 22 Lon C. Diehl/PhotoEdit, Inc.; p. 24 Brand X Pictures/Getty Images; p. 25 Caron Philippe/Corbis Sygma; p. 28 Jonathan Nourok/PhotoEdit, Inc.; p. 29 Allsport Concepts/Getty Images

Every effort has been made to contact copyright holders of any material reproduced in this book. Any omissions will be rectified in subsequent printings if notice is given to the publisher.

Contents

Some words are shown in bold, **like this.** You can find out what they mean by looking in the glossary.

What Is Safety?

It is important for everyone to stay safe.
Being safe means keeping out of danger.
It means staying away from things or
people that could hurt you.

Safety is important in everything you do. One good time to be safe is when you ride a bicycle. Bike riding can be fun if you are careful. Learning some rules about bicycles can help you stay safe.

Choosing a Bike

Bikes come in different sizes. You should choose a bike that is the right size for you. When you stand over the bar of the bike, your feet should be flat on the ground.

When you sit on the bike's seat, your toes should still touch the ground. Try different bikes until you find one that fits well.

Helmets

One important piece of safety **equipment** is a helmet. A helmet can **protect** your head if you fall. You can stay safe by wearing your helmet every time you ride.

Choose a helmet that fits tightly on the top of your head. Fasten the straps tightly under your chin. A loose helmet may not protect your head well.

Checking Your Equipment

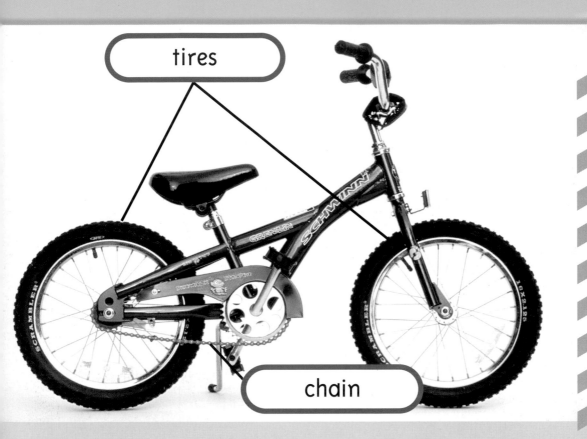

tires

chain

Before you ride, make sure your bicycle is working well. An adult can help you. The tires should have enough air. The brakes should help you stop smoothly. Tighten parts that have come loose.

If any parts are old or broken, get them fixed before you ride. You may also need to oil your bike's chain. Checking your **equipment** can help you stay safe.

Dressing for Safety

The right clothes can help you ride safely. Some clothes can get caught in the bike's chain. You should wear pants that are not too loose, and always tie your shoes.

If you ride near cars, wear bright colors so drivers can see you. When it gets dark, wear light colors or clothes with **reflectors.** Your bike should have lights and reflectors, too.

Safe Places to Ride

Bicycle riding takes lots of practice. You should always ride in safe places. Driveways, sidewalks, and empty parking lots can be good places to practice. Some parks also have bike paths.

When you ride, look where you are going. Watch for other riders and walkers. Call out or use a bell or horn to tell people you are coming. Then pass them on the left.

Rules of the Road

There are rules for riders on roads. Cars can hurt you because they are bigger. Bikes and cars can share the road safely by following some rules. Check the rules for riders where you live.

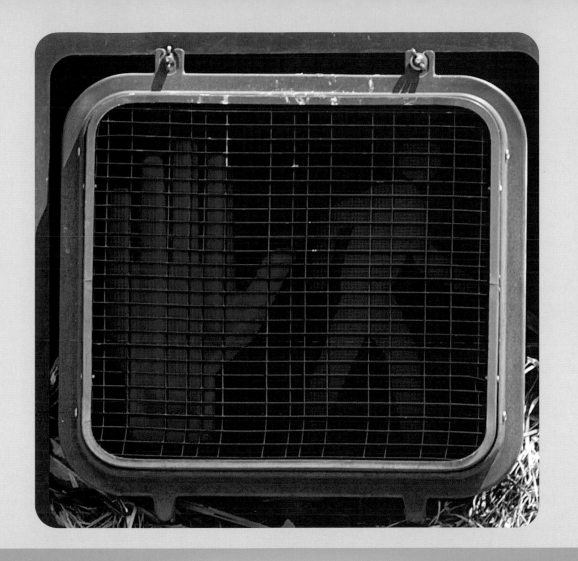

If you ride on a road, stay at the right side. Ride near the **curb** in **single file.** Pay attention to the road and the **traffic** around you. Obey the traffic lights and signs.

Hand Signals

left turn

Cars use lights to show when they want to stop or turn. Your hands can show this, too. When drivers see your **signals,** they should make room for you.

right turn

stop

Practice the hand signals at home. When you ride, show your signals before you need to stop or turn. This will give drivers a chance to slow down.

Crossing Streets

Be extra careful when you cross streets. Cross at a corner or crosswalk if you can. Stop your bike and look left, then right, then left again. Do not cross until the road is clear.

Walking with your bike is the safest way to cross. Walk quickly, but do not run, with the bike next to your right side. Watch for cars as you cross.

Dangers on the Road

Sometimes you may find problems on the road. Holes, puddles, and objects in the road can be unsafe. You should try to go around them if you can.

If the road is bumpy or rocky, ride slowly. This will keep your bike from **skidding** or falling. Ride slowly on hills, too, so you do not lose control of your bike.

Ride with Care

Make smart choices about safe places and times to ride. It is best to ride in the day if you can. Riding with a buddy can be fun and can help you stay safe.

Riding in bad weather is unsafe. If you get caught in rain or snow, walk your bike or ride slowly. Press the brakes gently to stop without **skidding** or falling.

If You Fall

Even careful riders sometimes fall. If you do, tell an adult. He or she can clean and treat your sores and check and fix your bike before you ride it again.

If you are badly hurt, stay still where you are. Ask your buddy or another person nearby to find help. An adult may need to call **911**.

Bicycle Fun

There are many fun things to do on your bicycle. You can see different plants and animals along nature trails. Join a bike club and ride with friends. You can even enter bike races.

No matter where you ride, you should be smart and careful. Following safety rules can keep you from getting hurt. Being safe will help you have fun!

Safety Tips

- Always ride safely. Do not try to show off.

- Wear your helmet every time you ride.

- Keep your hands on the handlebars. You can carry things in a basket or backpack.

- Only one person should ride a bike at a time. Do not give people rides on your bike.

- Lock your bike to a railing or bike rack when you finish riding. This may keep it from being stolen.

Glossary

911 phone number to dial in an emergency

buddy friend or partner

curb raised edge along the side of a street

equipment supply or machine used for a certain activity

protect keep safe

reflector something that shines back light

signal sign or movement used to show what will happen

single file in a line, one behind the other

skid slip or slide sideways or out of control

traffic cars and trucks moving along a road

Index